How to Attract A *R.E.A.L.* Man

10 Qualities R.E.A.L. Men Look For In A Woman

Bey Bright

iUniverse, Inc.
New York Bloomington

How To Attract A R.E.A.L. Man
10 Qualities R.E.A.L. Men Look For In a Woman

iUniverse books may be ordered through booksellers or by contacting:

iUniverse
1663 Liberty Drive
Bloomington, IN 47403
www.iuniverse.com
1-800-Authors (1-800-288-4677)

ISBN: 978-1-4401-3550-7 (sc)
ISBN: 978-1-4401-3551-4 (e-book)

Printed in the United States of America

iUniverse rev. date: 6/08/2009

Contents

Introduction

I've spoken to and have been involved with hundreds of women over the years and the overwhelming majority have suggested to me that they long for a "R.E.A.L."man. As a man, I had my own curiosities as to what these women really meant by suggesting they desire a "R.E.A.L."man. I've always asked myself the question, What is a "R.E.A.L."man in a woman's eyes? What qualities must a man possess for him to be considered a "R.E.A.L."man? What does a "R.E.A.L." man look like? What do "R.E.A.L."men act like? Do women themselves really even know what a "R.E.A.L."man is? I began to really listen, examine and investigate for myself what these women sought after so desperately. After logging thousands of hours of intimate, focused, and honest dialogue with the female persuasion of all races, educational backgrounds, and life experiences, I have concluded that the mass majority of women by their own admission desire a man to embody 4 key elements. The 4 key elements that most women feel they look for in a man are for him to be "Responsible, Educated, Ambitious, & Loving". In order to be happy and content within a relationship with a man, these 4 elements are the criteria that men must meet the majority of the time. Thus, I have created the acronym "R.E.A.L." to embody what women mean when they say they are looking for a "R.E.A.L."man. For years men have argued and debated with women about a woman's overall expectation level from a man and the type of commitment that would be necessary in order to have and maintain a successful relationship. In writing this book, it is my intended purpose to educate, enlighten, and entertain women from a "R.E.A.L."man's perspective on how to attract and attain a "R.E.A.L."man. I will share with you the valuable jewels of knowledge and wisdom of what it actually takes to achieve this goal if in fact you are sincere in your desires.

Why I Wrote This Book

I felt it was important to write this book because many people have lost their way emotionally and mentally in their relationships. It is my belief that the very essence of love and the foundation of quality, long lasting relationships are becoming a thing of the past. If you read many of the articles in today's popular magazines on the dynamics between men and women, most will have you believe that a strong, committed union between a man and woman is unnecessary and obsolete. I have put an emphasis on speaking and writing directly to and for women from a male perspective. I have in fact put the onus of saving male/female relationships and preserving the family structure primarily on the shoulders of women. I have chosen to do this because I sincerely believe that women are the ones capable of righting the ship so to speak and are the most naturally qualified to bring peace and harmony back to the relationship dynamic. As we delve deeper into how we may fix the problems that exist between men and women, it is my hope that women across the world truly embrace the philosophy shared in this book and use this book as a guide and a solution to truly come together in the spirit of cooperation. It is essential that men and women come together in a harmonious and productive way. Especially for the children. So many kids today are being born out of wedlock and the ramifications of men and women not remaining together are having dire consequences in every community across America and beyond. It is important to me as a man, a father, a husband, and productive member of society and community to educate and follow through on being a responsible person. Whether we realize it or not, we all stand to gain as a human race, a more prosperous quality of life when we teach our boys to become R.E.A.L. men and our young girls to become quality women. The following chapters will give complete insight on the 10 most important qualities "R.E.A.L."men look for in a woman.

PART ONE

The Qualities

Quality 1

Support His Dreams/ Understand His Vision

A "R.E.A.L." man worth having has a vision. He has a vision not only for himself, but for his children, his wife and everything pertaining to the overall success of his life. His direction or life path is usually based upon his life experiences, education and his dreams. He is the navigator of his ship and the captain. Please note: There are never 2 captains on a ship. There is however, a co-captain. It is in this role that a woman who wants a "R.E.A.L."man should learn to embrace. It is a complementary, yet vital role that will be loved, admired and respected by a "R.E.A.L."man. There are many times in life when a man's dreams and vision seem impractical, selfish, unrealistic, expensive, and downright foolish to a woman. In many cases, that may be the reality of the situation at certain points in a relationship. Many women reading this book now are probably saying "I've supported a man many times and got left holding the bag". "All those years of letting him "do him" got me nowhere". The problem was that your assessment of a "R.E.A.L."man was incorrect. What you did was waste years of valuable and precious time, love, energy, money and commitment on an immature, selfish, irresponsible, hateful, unfocused, ignorant, slacker of a male. The total antithesis of a "R.E.A.L."man!

Remember, "R.E.A.L." stands for "Responsible, Educated, Ambitious, & Loving" so those issues and concerns are obsolete. In order to attract and keep a "R.E.A.L." man, it is imperative that a woman realizes immediately that she must wholeheartedly support the dreams and embrace the vision of a "R.E.A.L."man or there is practically no chance of that relationship going the distance. By doing so, you will be greatly rewarded, appreciated and taken care of because that's what a "R.E.A.L. man will do for his woman! Understand that it is extremely difficult in today's world of marriages and relationships to sustain long term. I have seen in many instances where 2 people start off on the same page only to find that 5 years or so down the road that someone in the relationship comes to the realization they want change. Most of the time it is the woman who is unsatisfied within the relationship and wants out. Or so she thinks.

I have experienced this unfortunate situation in my own relationships over the course of my life and have found that the women who chose to leave wound up in far worse circumstances in terms of relationships than they had when we were a couple. They find out the hard way a R.E.A.L. man is a rare commodity in today's society. Being in a committed relationship has become more difficult in today's society. Especially for women in my opinion. Women today have more access than in any other time in history to better education, better jobs, greater pay, and the overall freedom to do, feel and think however they please. The woman of today has true and unadulterated liberation. However, along with that freedom and liberation there is still an underlying desire for many women to have a man in their life to complete their picture perfect exsistence. However, many women soon find that the type of man they are seeking, Responsible, Educated, Ambitious, and Loving have their own ideas of how they want their life to go. 9 times out of 10 these R.E.A.L. men have their own vision and dreams and are looking for a woman to compliment this process. Herein lies the dilemma and lack of understanding for most women. They are finding out that they really do not want to compromise and buy into a man's way of doing things. They prefer to do it their way and find that compromise and complementary roles are not suitable. The realities from a R.E.A.L. man's perspective are this. If you do not feel that his vision of life is where you see yourself and you are unwilling to support his dream, my advice would be to prepare to fly solo or get yourself a guppy! If you are the type of woman who can roll with the program, it shows us that you are totally committed to us and to what we can build together. It also shows us that you possess another one of the 10 qualities we look for in a woman (maybe the most important) which is LOYALTY as discussed next in the book.

Quality 2

Loyalty

Maybe the most important and valuable quality a woman can possess in the eyes of a "R.E.A.L." man is that of loyalty. It is the very foundation upon which everything is built and the essence of what can be attained, achieved and preserved in the mind and heart of a "R.E.A.L." man. For those women who may be unsure as to what the definition of loyalty is, let me give the basic and intangible definitions to alleviate any confusion. Loyalty by standard definition is defined as faithfulness to commitments and obligations. It also means a feeling of devoted attachment and affection. Loyalty is important to many people but particularly to a "R.E.A.L." man because of life's many obstacles and struggles. Trying to achieve and maintain certain goals and status, whether it be economical, educational or professional is usually a daunting task in this dog eat dog world in which we all live. The woman who truly professes and shows loyalty to the "R.E.A.L." man, especially when the chips are down, is the one who reaps the benefits of a solid and rewarding relationship. Another term used to describe this type of woman is called a "Ride or Die Chick" as affectionately defined by the hip hop generation. This type of woman will forsake all of her nay saying girlfriends and family members when that "R.E.A.L." man goes out on a limb and throws caution to the wind in pursuit of his true dreams and ambitions. The scenario may be of an entrepreneurial nature whereas your man may be making a six figure income (or more) and you all are living "The American Dream" as they say. However, your man is feeling stymied in his current working environment and really feels the need to explore his underlying passions in which the outcome of his endeavor may be unknown. Thus, upsetting the applecart so to speak and the level of comfort in which you've grown accustomed to. Ask yourself ladies, what do you do? Do you become a source of negative energy in which you become a naysayer consumed with doubts and fears? Do you become selfish to the point in which you feel that his need to take risks and pursue his dreams will have an adverse effect on you and your social standing amongst your friends and associates therefore causing you to not be supportive? Remember what Quality 1 was? "Support His Dreams/Understand His Vision. In many aspects, there is a direct correlation between loyalties and supporting the dreams of a "R.E.A.L." man based on the premise that in order to actually be supportive of a man's vision and dreams, you have to many times be physically, emotionally and sometimes financially vested in that man which in fact is a show of loyalty in and of itself. In speaking with many women, the subject of loyalty and what it means to a "R.E.A.L." man and what it means to a woman is always controversial and usually a source of frustration that many times lead to arguments, resentment and oftentimes, eventual breakups.

My words of wisdom to a woman looking for a relationship with a "R.E.A.L." man are that the loyalty factor is Non Negotiable! Either you have it in you to roll with the punches or you don't. "R.E.A.L." men understand a woman's need for security and that it is usually their number one priority. It's in their DNA. However, it is imperative to remember that "R.E.A.L." stands for Responsible, Educated, Ambitious, and Loving" so although risks will more than likely be taken, the "R.E.A.L." man will always take you and his family's well being into account. Thus, displaying his loyalty to you! It's in *HIS* DNA! Some great examples of love, loyalty and success are (1) Nancy and Ronald Reagan, (2) Coretta and Martin Luther King Jr. (3) Hillary and Bill Clinton, (4) Bonnie and Clyde (5) Carmella and Vito Corleone, (6) Valarie Simpson and Nick Ashford. (7) Rachel and Jackie Robinson, (8) Maria Shriver and Arnold Schwarzenegger. (9) Michelle and Barack Obama. Just to reiterate, I am not suggesting that the aforementioned relationships were perfect. However, I believe there can be little debate about the amount of success, loyalty, love, and commitment each woman noted has demonstrated to her husband for the entire world to see. As the old saying goes; "Behind the success of every great man is a great woman!" Enough said!

Quality 3

Be a Nurturer

Being a nurturer; is this an innate quality that all women have and are born with? Can this important quality be learned or taught at some point and time throughout a woman's life? I cannot say unequivocally that I have the true answer to that question. However, myself and most "R.E.A.L." men I know and have spoken to believe it is a God given instinct that is a woman's most precious gift. The basic definition of nurture is to support and encourage. The quality and ability of a woman to be a nurturer is of colossal importance to a "R.E.A.L." man because it indicates a certain level of character or a lack thereof. A "R.E.A.L." man needs to be certain that his children and home environment will be loved and provided for by his woman and that those issues will be her first priorities and general focus. (For all you women who make running out to the clubs and hanging out all night every night at the expense of the kids your number one priority, please consider yourselves not the one for a "R.E.A.L." man) He also wants to know and feel that his own personal needs, both emotional and physical will be met. In recent years, today's "modern woman", the highly educated, career oriented, highly compensated and world traveled has seemingly lost touch with her nurturing abilities and her capacity to relate to men on a whole with regards to relationships. Whether or not this is a conscious decision on a woman's part is a subject of debate and to be honest, inconsequential. The hard line truth of the matter is unless this "modern woman" is a nurturer, who really embodies the quality of "Self Sacrifice" which I touch on later on in the book; a "R.E.A.L." man will not be interested in you! Let me repeat this, "Will Not Be Interested in YOU! I can hear you women now cussing and fussing saying "He has some damn nerve!" Many women I've spoken to about this really take offense with me over this subject because they see it as a slight to their achievements and many assume that there is some sort of an inferiority complex or jealously attached to this philosophy. Ladies, do all of us "R.E.A.L." men a favor, "GET OVER YOURSELVES!" Let me break it down to you like this. Do you really think a "Responsible", a man handling his business, "Educated", a man that has a college degree, world traveled and street smart, "Ambitious", a total go-getter and achiever, and "Loving", a quality character and affectionate guy that along with those other 3 traits has it going on so much that he probably has to turn women away could really feel inferior or jealous of you? That's ludicrous! Although there are many valid reasons, explanations and scenarios as to why women's behavior and thought processes towards men have changed over the years, one thing has not changed and will never change. A "R.E.A.L." man aka the "ALPHA MALE" will always be and see himself as leader and El Captain.

One theory many "R.E.A.L./ALPHA" men have is that with all the absentee fathers, metro sexual, homosexual and bisexual men running around in society today, many women don't know what a R.E.A.L./ALPHA male is or how to respect and relate to one when they encounter one. In turn, this societal phenomenon has "modern women" in fact possessing and desiring to have the very same characteristics that are historically found in the alpha male, thus creating an imbalance and a lack of healthy, committed relationships. Though many women argue with men like me who embrace this philosophy, it is evident that while many achievements are being made by many of today's "modern women" of all races and backgrounds, there have been severe repercussions that have adversely affected women because many are going against in my opinion, the natural makeup of a woman, that of a nurturer. It comes as no surprise that those women who suppress and ignore their nurturing abilities to concentrate solely on their corporate and educational ambitions, tend to be the women who by age 35 become depressed, lonely, angry, frustrated, disillusioned and bitter. There are however, *some* exceptions to these findings. If you take a real close and honest look at past generations of couples who were together for 30, 40, 50 years and speak to the women in those relationships I believe you would find two main things. One, that most of those women will admit that it was not always easy and many sacrifices, many of them personal were made. Second, most of those women took pride and a sense of accomplishment in the fact they raised, nurtured and were the foundations of families and children who became productive members of society. These women also enjoyed a love and partnership full of good times with a man that many of today's "modern women" will never experience because they don't recognize the value in possessing the quality of the "Nurturer". Many "R.E.A.L." men usually have a great mother or grandmother who raised and nurtured them and helped them become the "R.E.A.L." men they are today. But, "don't get it twisted" as the saying goes. A "R.E.A.L." man never wants a second mother for a wife. Even though, many women I've spoken to would disagree! It is important to understand that a wife becomes the natural extension of a great mom because she will possess many of the qualities "R.E.A.L." men have come to know and respect. There is a big difference between a "mama's boy" and a man who loves and respects his mother. After all, you know what they say, a man who doesn't have a healthy love and respect for his mother, will never have a healthy and loving relationship with a woman. Keep this in mind ladies!

Quality 4

Self Sacrificing

What does it mean to self sacrifice? Why is it important to a "R.E.A.L." man for a woman to be self sacrificing? Self sacrifice to a "R.E.A.L." man basically means to put the needs of others, particularly the children and husband, before your own *instinctively*. I believe that this quality is a natural extension of being a "NURTURER" as it most times finds a good woman making sure the needs of her family are attended to first. Many times, it's just the little things a woman will do that make "R.E.A.L." men take notice. Making sure the kids are properly fed and their homework is done correctly in the evening. Even when your favorite television show is on and you are dead dog tired, the woman who can dig deep within herself to make sure her family is straight is the type of woman a "R.E.A.L." man wants to have in his life. He respects the type of woman that gets up early in the morning to feed the family breakfast or stays up late at night to prepare the kids lunch for school. He admires the kind of woman who gets up in the middle of the night to feed the baby and changes the baby's diaper. He desires the kind of woman that when her man has an important job interview or major presentation at work, she looks to make sure his suit, shirt and tie are just right. Many of today's "modern women" feel that it's all about them and their own personal wants and desires. I will be the first to agree that a person should be able to pursue their passions and do whatever makes them happy. (Within reason & legally) However, since the book is intended to be an honest guide into the minds of "R.E.A.L." men, I'm telling all the ladies point blank that if you feel the need to put yourself and your gratifications first, you will *NEVER* be the one for a "R.E.A.L." man. As life becomes more hectic for many of us today, the will and desire to self sacrifice for someone else's benefit becomes more and more difficult and a daunting task to say the least. I think back to a time when mothers and grandmothers would and could do a variety of tasks that were both tedious and tiresome all for the benefit of their family. Many of the "modern women" I speak to today speak as though their lives are so much more demanding than those women of generations past. Many women I have spoken to truly feel as though because we are living in a new era of exsistence that it may have in fact been easier for women of past generations to be self sacrificing. I strongly disagree with that sentiment. In fact, there is evidence to suggest that living conditions and life in general was harder for most people and by default much more difficult for women. Yet in still, many women of the past seemed better conditioned mentally, emotionally and physically to sacrifice and endure the rigors of life. They understood and took pride in the fact that they were the foundations for their families and that their many sacrifices would benefit the entire family one hundred fold. It is unfortunate to see that we as a society have become extremely self centered and overindulgent to the point that the lack of self sacrifice is having a detrimental effect on society at large. Once women stop sacrificing, all is lost.

Quality 5

Be a Lady

Wow! What do I mean by "be a lady"? This should be obvious but surprisingly, I've found myself having to explain the exact definition to many women as to what a "R.E.A.L." man considers lady like behavior. First of all, it's all in the way a woman carries herself. Everything from the way she speaks, dresses, walks, and behaves, particularly in social settings will determine if you are the type of woman "R.E.A.L." men would consider for a serious, committed relationship. A lady by definition is feminine, polite, refined and well spoken. She is an object of chivalrous devotion. This may sound corny and old fashion but one of the most important lessons I try to get across to women is that most men never change. We have an image in our head and an innate belief about what a wife and mother should be and act like. It may be a false sense of ideological beliefs that many men have buried deep into their psyche. However, as the saying goes; "it is what it is". You will hear me say many times in this book that I am not here to argue and debate with people about why. I am writing and sharing with you about the realities of "what is". There are many women who feel like men have a sense of hypocrisy about what they really want from women along with their genuine likes and dislikes. Guess what ladies? You are absolutely correct. Most men have a difficult time being true to themselves about who they really are and about what they want and expect from the woman in their life. As I discussed earlier in the book, most men are really looking for a woman who possesses those external "wholesome" qualities that a good mother or grandmother display in that man's childhood. Notice I said "external wholesome qualities". Surely as we men get older we come to the harsh realities that behind closed doors on "grown up" time, mom and grandma were getting their groove on and enjoying the same sexual escapades that many men brag about to their boys about other women. This is part of the hypocrisy that exists in a man's makeup and part of the deep denial that lives within all men. Some of us eventually come to terms with this denial and embrace the truth about the complex nature of a woman. I'll leave you with this point about being a lady. Men want a *lady* in the streets but a freak in the bed! Enough said!

Quality 6

Be a Good Cook

Ladies, you already know this fact. The fastest and best way to a man's heart is through his stomach! If this is indeed the reality, can someone please explain to me why in the hell so many women either refuse or more shockingly don't know how to cook? This growing phenomenon is at critical mass and high alert, especially between the age groups of 18 to 45, the so called "modern woman era". What I find even more alarming is that some of these women have children and can't even cook! This has to be one of the biggest turnoffs to a "R.E.A.L." man. The fact that a woman cannot cook or refuses to is a sign and character trait a "R.E.A.L." man can and will do without. Trust me on this! Don't let these new jack, metrosexual, homosexual men convince you that it's all good to go out to eat 3 to 4 times a week. Any man who is down for that program I guarantee does not fit the "R.E.A.L." man profile. He's the type of man who will be looking to go dutch everytime you go out to a restaurant! See how fast you ladies get tired of that program! Most guys love it when the holidays come around and we look forward to having all those home cooked meals which smell so delicious it makes your mouth water! We think about how our mom and grandma used to make our favorite dishes, whether it be baked chicken, macaroni and cheese, candied yams, honey baked ham, mashed potatoes or apple pie. It gave you a warm feeling inside and that food also symbolized a sense of love. A love for family, a love for friends, a love of togetherness, and definitely a love to eat! I think back to that classic movie Soul Food and the character of Big Mama. That movie exemplifies exactly what being a good cook is all about and the underlying psychology behind the importance of cooking for your man and your family. Though many of today's young women dont want to admit this to themselves, the fact of the matter is they have become extremely selfish, lazy and self centered. I don't even like using the term lazy with regards to the cooking matter primarily because these women have the energy and desire to do whatever else it is they want to do. It just so happens that most of the young women today don't have the energy and desire to cook or to even learn how. What most men R.E.A.L. or not do know is this, today's young women love to eat! They damn sure don't mind putting their feet under a table ready to chow down on a five course meal. They also don't mind calling all over town during a holiday like Memorial Day, or the 4th of July looking for the nearest barbeque and picnic they can run to. They just want to sit back, chill, be fed, drink and socialize.

What the hell is that all about! Like I always say, the game and the times may change, put human nature will always remain the same. If any woman reading this book is interested in having a relationship with a R.E.A.L. man, you may want to put down the E Lynn Harris books and pick up a few cookbooks! Bon Appetit!

Quality 7

Be a Listener

I believe that most people are self interested and self absorbed which leads to most individuals being concerned with their own self interests. This quality in people usually means they are always talking and never listening. Being a listener is a very important quality that a "R.E.A.L." man looks for in a woman. Especially ones we want to get serious with. It is a rare quality in people let alone a woman because most women love to communicate and have their feelings acknowledged along with getting their point across. However, many "R.E.A.L." men who are looking to build for the future and have a life vision are turned off by women who are only concerned with themselves and never take into consideration what he is communicating. In order for that woman to be recognized as that solid foundation, a woman who wants to attract a "R.E.A.L." man must have the ability to listen and convince that "R.E.A.L." man the needs of he and his children will be understood and met to the best of her abilities. The best women are great listeners and know what their man and children need without them having to utter one single word. Most times, a great woman knows what her man needs before he does! It's not enough just to hear us, we need for you to comprehend and give us intelligent feedback on what we are trying to communicate. Nothing is more frustrating than when you are trying to explain something to a woman or when something good happens to you that you are excited to share and she is totally nonchalant and inattentive. That really ticks us off and gives us reason to believe we can't share our most intimate details with you due to your seeming lack of interest. Many times the inability of a woman to be a good listener can also lead to affairs and infidelity on the part of many men. I think one of the biggest misconceptions out there is that a man does not want or need to have his feelings acknowleged. This is so far from the truth. In fact, it is a necessity that the feelings of R.E.A.L. men and what we are trying to convey be taken seriously and given the proper consideration. Although some men may have difficulties with direct verbal communication, if you are an attentive woman you can usually understand what we are trying to say and what we are looking for. Here are a few words of wisdom ladies. As my grandmother used to say, talk less and listen more. Be a listener!

Quality 8

Have a Sense of Humor

Have you ever heard the expression "don't take yourself so seriously?" A "R.E.A.L." man enjoys a woman who knows how to laugh and have a good time and who is not overly pretentous. Any woman who does not know how to take a joke, tell a joke and cannot blend in comfortably within that man's inner circle will most likely not be chosen as "the one". Having a sense of humor about things oftentimes tells a lot about a person. Humor is defined as the faculty of perceiving what is comical or amusing. Although no one is suggesting a woman needs to be a clown either. A happy balance and a good amount of humor is a wonderful and fun way to keep a relationship healthy and built to last for the long haul. Laughter is good for the spirit and soul so try to yuk it up every once and a while and be as light hearted as possible. Most people like to keep things light and have a difficult time coping with individuals they perceive as being "too heavy". Again, the "R.E.A.L." man understands that problems will most certainly arise in any relationship. The "R.E.A.L." man also understands how to provide love, support and comfort to help ease the pain during those trying times. However, this section is about having a sense of humor. I know with much certainty that the majority of women love a man who can make her laugh. Although laughing and having a sense of humor may not be at the very top of a "R.E.A.L." man's list, it is still one of the main essentials to have! Many men I have spoken to in general while writing this book pointed out a few famously funny women that they said seemed to be cool and easy to get along with. They seem to enjoy the spirit, humor, and light heartedness of Ellen Degeneres, Tracey Ellis Ross, Whoopi Goldberg, Jennifer Aniston, Nicole Kidman, Selma Hayak, Heidi Klum, Kelly Ripka, Taraji Henson and Beyonce Knowles-Carter. It seems as if all these women have a pleasant and cooperative spirit and enjoy being in a committed relationship. Oh, did I forget to mention that these women also have very successful careers!

Quality 9

Have a Hobby

Truth be told ladies, most men do not enjoy the regularity of being in a woman's company (unless of course it's in a sexual capacity) due to the simple fact we just don't share enough of the same common interest. Most women love being with their man but find what we like to do boring with a capital B! Things like playing golf and basketball, going fishing and hunting, discussing politics, watching football all day on Sunday grate on the nerves of most women. Watching Project Runway, HGTV, The Bachelor, Judge Everybody, Oprah & America's Next Top Model everyday will drive a man to the brink of insanity! Many women have told me that they find men to be downright obsessive in their behavior towards the things they enjoy doing the most. And guess what ladies, I have the solution to your problem. GET A HOBBY! While a R.E.A.L. man will always attempt to give his woman adequate and quality time, he needs his personal space and freedom to unwind. Recognizing that our so called obsessions have become a source of irritation for many of our women, to keep the balance of the relationship healthy we R.E.A.L. men love it when you hang out with your sisters, girlfriends, mother and sorority mates. We encourage you to join a bookclub, attend church activities or whatever it is you enjoy doing. Just know that R.E.A.L. men prefer that their woman is doing something other than nagging them about God knows what all day everyday! It is always good for a woman to have a hobby and engage in something that she can call her own within the relationship. I have had many women tell me that engaging in a variety of activities and hobbies has helped to boost their self esteem and invigorate their sense of spirit and commitment to their relationship. Most experienced individuals who have been in committed relationships will tell you that having a hobby separate from one another is the best thing you can do to actually enhance your relationship. Besides, when the game is on and there's 10 seconds left in the 4th quarter, it's 4th and goal at the 5 yard line, no timeouts, and his team needs a touchdown to tie... Oh no! They scored and went into overtime! Better get a hobby ladies! (smile)

Quality 10

Honesty

Do you remember when you were a kid and you were afraid to admit and confess to something you did wrong or by mistake to your parents or teacher? Do you remember what they used to tell you? They used to say that honesty is the best policy. That little quality called honesty will make or break a relationship every time. Let's face it. Who wants to be in a relationship with a person who is totally dishonest and always lying about even the most miniscule of things. To a R.E.A.L. man, nothing is more intolerable than a deceitful woman. So much is built around the woman that a R.E.A.L. man chooses that it becomes absolutely imperative for his woman to possess the honesty and high moral character it requires for this R.E.A.L. man to realize his total success and potential. As I stated earlier in the book, behind every great man stands a great woman. No person can ever be truly great without a strong sense of character and moral conviction. It is my belief that the character trait of honesty is even more important for a woman to possess because of how it can affect so many other of the qualities that would make a woman great, thus causing a total imbalance. Let me explain. When a woman is dishonest by nature, it then affects her ability to be a good nurturer, it makes her disloyal, and causes her to make decisions and exemplify actions that would be deemed unlady like. When a man is Responsible, Educated, Ambitious, and Loving, he expects to be able to trust his woman with the household finances and the rearing of the children. He also expects his woman to be able to truthfully communicate her needs, dreams, and ambitions so that he may remain aware and recognize what is of importance to her. Honesty by defintion is described as truthfulness, sincerity, and frankness. I realize that no one is perfect and that some people withhold certain things from their spouse in the name of protecting that person's feelings or maybe even due to a fear of rejection. However, this is no excuse for you not to be as honest as you possibly can be in your relationships. It is always a risk in being totally honest with the ones you love and never easy to do. All in all, honesty is the best policy.

PART TWO

The Commentary

Commentary 1

Sexual Compatability

I have to speak on a unique quality that R.E.A.L. men sometimes look for in a woman that didn't quite make the top ten of my list. However, I believe it was important enough to discuss in commentary. That quality is sexual compatability. Now this quality is somewhat controversial because to the many women I have spoken to, they have suggested to me that most men are extremely insecure and become afraid when a woman displays her true sexual prowess and appetite. In all honesty, I have talked to alot of men and I'm ashamed to admit it ladies but, you are correct in your assessment of most men. However, we are not talking about most men. We are focusing on the R.E.A.L. man! This man possesses the self confidence, communication skills, and experience to handle whatever sexual scenario you throw at him. It is imperative that a R.E.A.L. man finds a woman who is willing to satisfy ALL of his sexual needs and desires or that woman runs the high risk of facing excessive infidelity on behalf of her man. The real hard line truth is that any woman who is too sexually reserved, selfish, or just unwilling to "make it happen" in the bedroom on a consistent basis, will more than likely be ruled out. If a man loves receiving oral sex and a woman only wants to perform it only when there is a solar eclipse, and is half heartedly performing at that, chances are you will be ruled out or stepped out on from time to time! I really try not to overemphasize the total importance of this particular quality due to the fact the other qualities mentioned in this book usually carry more weight in a R.E.A.L. man's decision making process for choosing the woman he decides to make his wife or main woman. There have been many debates about monogamy and the overall realities regarding that practice. It has been examined for centuries and spoken upon from the perspective of religious groups, scientists, and people who study the animal kingdom and all have drawn their own conclusions about the subject. I don't want to even go down the road of discussing monogamy and the beliefs of it in detail because that discussion and debate is another book all together in itself! However, I acknowleged its purpose to safeguard against the viewpoint of those many women I have interviewed and encountered who suggest that it doesn't matter how great or terrible a woman is in and out of the bedroom because most men are inclined to cheat anyway. I am not here to debate whether or not that premise is true or untrue but to state the point that it becomes less likely and more infrequent that a man will stray sexually if he and his woman share an honest and open sexual compatability. I always say and will stand by the fact that men are the easiest creatures to figure out. We are all first and foremost visual beings. We are aroused initially by how that woman looks. It is not necessarily about physical beauty either. It's mostly about what you are wearing and how you are wearing it. It is about how your hair is styled.

It could be about the color nail polish on your hands and feet to the type of lingerie you wear to bed at night. For many men however, it is all about sex appeal. I've seen less attractive women look and be more sexy than a woman with natural beauty. It is absolutely mind boggling. Many times you will find that a man may be having affairs or infidelities with women who are not as physically fit or attractive as their wives or girlfriends. Many women take their personal appearance for granted when they get into a marriage or committed relationship. I have known and interviewed numerous women who suggest that they dress for themselves and not for their man. They are only concerned about what they like to wear and the style of dress they feel most comfortable in. Ladies, let me tell you point blank that this type of attitude is bound to cause you trouble in your relationship. It all kind of gets back to being that certain kind of woman with those certain qualities I speak about in this book. It is really up to you as a woman as to how important it is for you to be sexually compatible with your man.

Commentary 2

Daddy's Little Girl

Most women who grow up with a loving father in the household and brag about being a "daddy's girl" are in for a rude awakening when dealing with men and relationships. They are under the unfortunate misconception that their man will treat them like their daddy treated them; with *unconditional love!* What many women fail to realize and eventually find out is that a father's unconditional love can never be replicated nor should it be expected from another man. Everything in life has conditions and relationships are no different. What that daddy's girl also fails to realize is her relationship with her father for many years is generally one sided. Meaning, daddy is the one always providing, loving and giving while you are mainly the recipient of all of these wonderful things. Whether it was giving you money for that new bag, those expensive shoes, your first car, college expenses, taking care of your emotional needs and insecurities or whatever else your little heart desired, daddy was your go to guy. I am not here suggesting that you are a bad person or that you did anything wrong here either. Most R.E.A.L. men who have daughters are more than happy to do any and everything they can do to ensure their daughter's happiness and well being. I'm just saying that a woman's transition from daddy to boyfriend or husband is an extremely different dynamic and one that tends to throw many women for a loop because their expectation levels within that relationship with a man are unrealistic. The spoiled and selfish little daddy's girl does not play well with a R.E.A.L. man or any type of man for that matter. I encourage all daddy's girls looking to find true happiness and contentment to contemplate and honestly examine what I have just outlined. It is my true belief that once you can come to terms and understand that the dynamics of your relationship with your father and another man will be totally different based on the understanding that in your relationship with daddy, you are the main recipient. When you enter into a relationship with a man be it boyfriend or husband, you in fact have to become more of a giver in every facet of the relationship. There must be a healthy balance established in a relationship between a man and a woman. Once established, that relationship has a solid chance to blossom and prosper! So many women become disillusioned when they find out that most men will never live up to who their daddy was and to what he was able to provide for you in all facets of your life. The key is to look for those certain good qualities in a man that remind you of your dad without expecting him to *be* your dad. I know that may be difficult for some of you ladies but it is a must! Just like a man cannot and should not expect his woman to be his mama or grandmother, the same rules apply to you!

Commentary 3

The Guppy and The Barracuda

Many successful and well educated women have told me that they are looking for a man that is their equal but admit they are having the hardest time finding that fulfilling, long term relationship they seek. They suggest that they are looking for that Harvard educated, Wall Street broker type guy. The mover and the shaker! The fearless conqueror! The sexual mandingo stallion! In other words, they're looking for the barracuda. But what they really need is a guppy! If I had a dollar for everytime a woman told me that the nice guy who did everything for her was boring and not her type, I'd be a rich man! It always puzzuled me as a youth as to why the nice guys almost always finished last. I guess having a man who treats you like shit is exciting! The man who never calls you, never remembers your birthday, abuses you, never takes you anywhere and stands you up is every woman's fantasy. Right? The terms "guppy and barracuda" are terms I've chosen to use to describe two main personality types of men. Although both can be deemed as extreme characteristics of a man's nature and are on totally opposite sides of the spectrum, it is important to examine and comprehend why it is essential that a woman knows if she needs or desires a barracuda or a guppy type. A barracuda type man usually fits the description of one who is highly successful, charismatic, selfish, arrogant, conceited, shallow, cocky, sexually gratifying and predatory. Guess what ladies? For most of you, whether you want to admit this or not, all these qualities turn you on and are synonomous with EXCITEMENT to most of you! The characteristics of the guppy type man are non aggressive, non confrontational, overly accomodating, extremely generous, uncharismatic, predictable, average, uncomplicated, needy, and sexually reluctant. Guess what ladies? For most of you, whether you want to admit this or not, are turned off by the very sound of these qualities and identify these characteristics as BORING! However, what most women fail to realize, especially the dominate, aggressive and controlling types is that they'd be more compatible with a "guppy type" of man for the long haul. What I try to get many women to realize is that they need to be with a man who is opposite of their temperment and personality type. Simply put, if you're an aggressive, bossy type, you need a man who is easy going and very open to taking instruction and critique. If you are a woman who is more meek in nature, you should seek a man who naturally takes command and provides the energy necessary all the while complimenting you. If women do not embrace this reality, there will continue to be a constant clash in your relationships and we all know how volatile things can get in relationships between two strong willed individuals. Things often go to the point of no return whereas things are said and actions are taken that more times than not are deemed as unforgivable or deal breakers.

In all honesty ladies, my theory about the barracuda and guppy brings us back to the my earlier statements in the book about understanding the alpha male and what he is naturally inclined to do, feel, accept and not accept. The same can now actually be said for the alpha female and to whom this book was really intended to reach. Would you like to know who really is to blame for the imbalance that exists between male/female relationships over the last 20 years? Babyface, the Ultimate Guppy! It was Babyface the singer who in 1989, upset the apple cart and had his guppy songs resonating with women all over America. Songs like Soon As I Get Home and Whip Appeal although great songs, sent a message that go against the traditional grain of the alpha male. Most men and women would admit if they are honest with themselves that in the relationship between Tracy Edmonds and Babyface that Babyface was the guppy aka the "non alpha male" and Tracy was the barracuda aka the "alpha female". But here is the main point. That marriage lasted for at least a decade so my theory of the guppy and barracuda stands true. The alpha male and alpha female cannot and will not co-exist in harmony for any real length of time. It's an impossibilty. I had a funny vision one day and I'd like to share it with you ladies. The vision I had I named "The Motorcycle Effect". I would like all of today's "modern women" to ponder this. Picture a couple going for a ride on a sporty Harley-Davidson motorcycle on a crisp, cool, autumn day down the countryside. Now envision a tall, dark and handsome man riding with you on that motorcycle.. with you driving and that man on the back of the motorcycle with his arms securely wrapped around your waist with his sweater tied around his neck! Most women, if they're honest, find that picture downright repulsive and a complete turn off. Can you imagine seeing a Michael Jordan or George Clooney in that role? Ain't gonna happen! Sorry ladies. The motorcycle effect is a microcosm of where I see society and the male/female relationship going. The alpha male and R.E.A.L. man will NEVER subject himself to this state of unnatural behavior! Like my girl Taraji Henson said in the movie Baby Boy, "Please believe me"! Do yourselves a favor my bold, beautiful alpha women! Get yourselves a guppy and live happily ever after!

Commentary 4

A Woman's Two Biggest Fears

As I have stated before, I have personally been involved with hundreds of women in my time as a single man, although I am now a married man. I have studied in a very intimate and psychological manner what makes women tick so to speak. I grew up in a single parent household in which I was raised by my mother. I grew up in a family that was dominated and run by women. Unfortunately, the R.E.A.L. men I speak about and the qualities they possess were for the most part absent in my life so like many young boys with the same experience, we all pretty much see and hear the same things play out in our lives and very few of us can process and communicate the effects it has on our male psyche. Over the years, I have tried to understand what I had also internalized as a boy and young man with regards to the women in my life and what I saw was bringing them mental anguish and frustration from the male partners in their lives. From my grandmother, aunts, girl cousins, girlfriends, wife, to my own mother I became able to identify the two biggest fears of all women. The two biggest fears of a woman are BOREDOM and The LACK of SECURITY. Security and excitement come in many different forms. It can be emotional, financial, mental etc. It is important to think about these fears in the broadest of spectrums and not limit it to one or two things. Think about it ladies, when you complain about something with regards to your man it usually revolves around the fact you think he's not handling his business to your particular satisfaction. He's unemployed or the job he has doesn't cut the mustard in your opinion. That speaks to your feelings of security or the lack thereof. The feeling that he will not be able to provide for you and your children in the manner in which it has been mapped out in your head or maybe you've grown accustomed to by being a "daddy's girl". If you find yourself constantly telling your man to make plans for you both to go somewhere together or you want him to think of something on his own for you both to do but he never does. The reason you don't want to have sex with your man regularly because he only wants you in the missionary position, is old fashioned, a 2 minute man, and fails to explore your mind, body and soul to give you that erotic and orgasmic experience you crave speaks to the boredom you will feel as a woman. I know that many woman recognize and some have even acknowledged these issues to themselves, their girlfriends and sometimes even their man. But have you women acknowledged that these are actually two fears that consume your very existence and essentially make up who you are as people? The reality is that men are not built to operate around the fear of being bored and secure. This is evident by the fact most men will eat the same meat and potatoes dinner for a week straight with no complaint.

Many men will risk having an affair, take most of the his savings and risk it on his entrepreneurial dreams and a host of other things because for the most part men do not have an immediate fear of lack of security and usually don't get bored very easily. For the most part, men are total creatures of habit and women are creatures of change. My advice to the ladies would be to find a man who keeps you entertained mentally, physically and sexually to alleviate the risk of being bored. Also, I suggest finding a man who has enough financial resources, communication skills, and emotional strength to meet your personal comfort level and can satisfy your inate need for security.

Commentary 5

Realistic Expectations

The whole reason for me writing this book was not and most certainly is not to demean or belittle women. Let me reiterate that point and be very clear about that. My intentions are to help you all get a better understanding of how most men really think, feel and behave with regards to how they pick and choose a woman. Whether it's choosing a woman to be a wife or just to have casual relations, there is always a method to the madness. Especially when it comes to dealing with the R.E.A.L. man. This blunt commentary touches on the importance of a woman having realistic expectations when it comes to dealing with a R.E.A.L. man. While you should always be confident in your abilities and never be afraid to go after what you desire, you should understand that attracting and being in a committed relationship with a R.E.A.L. man requires for you to have your stuff together and certain things about yourself already in tact. Things like the 10 qualities we've discussed already in this book!

Think about it, it's like a person wanting to have a career as a gourmet chef in a 5 star restaurant and that person never learned how to cook. It's a totally unrealistic fantasy. Right? Don't expect to be with a R.E.A.L. man when you do not possess at least 8 of the 10 qualities discussed in this book. I can guarantee you that you will fail in your attempts to have this man in any long term commitment. You need to see what great qualities you already possess along with the ones you do not. Maybe you have some of the qualities but have not yet perfected them enough to make that R.E.A.L. man a believer. You need to ask yourself, what can I bring to this R.E.A.L. man's world that will be of value to him that he is bound to appreciate? It would be unrealistic to think you can have things be all about you and your desires. It would be unrealistic to think that you never will be asked to compromise or give up something in order to make things work between you and that R.E.A.L.man. Ladies, meeting and being in a strong, committed relationship with a quality man is almost like finding and getting your dream job. It requires preparation, self discipline, creativity, and enthusiasm. Most women are not prepared when they think they have found the guy *they* want to be with. I have known some women to think that just because they are pretty plus sexually dynamic in bed that that should be enough. I remember one woman I was seeing suggested to me that the fact that she was great at giving oral sex should justify her not having to know how to cook, nurture, or have anything else I felt I needed. She sincerely believed we could have a serious relationship! Sorry ladies! I'm here to tell you that all you can and should expect from having just those physical attributes to offer a R.E.A.L. man are constant booty calls on the late night creep. If you are extremely lucky, an occasional dinner and movie. I know it sounds extremely harsh but I'm not here to candy coat anything for you ladies. It is imperative to have realistic expectations when dealing with R.E.A.L. men. If you take my advice to heart, I am confident you will find and get what you are looking for more times than not.

Commentary 6

The Plain Jane Theory

Isn't it amazing that more and more you are seeing great looking guys walking hand and hand with the "average woman"? And vice versa. It has become more and more rare to see that "A" list power couple together these days. Ask yourself, how many Brad Pitt and Angelina Jolie couples do you see walking down the street side by side? Shouldn't a Denzel Washington "type" of man be with a Halle Berry "type" of woman? I can't tell you when was the last time I've seen a truly striking couple out on the town together. Many of you "sophisticated ladies" reading this book may not want to admit it but you've all wondered to yourselves or even said to your girlfriend at one time or another, "Damn that guy is fine!" "What's a fine man like that doing with a woman like her?" It seems like such a phenomenon these days but in reality, maybe it was always this way to a general extent. Maybe R.E.A.L. men who happen to also be "fine" prefer to be with what I like to call "The Plain Jane". There have been many songs over the years

47

which even suggest that it might be more beneficial for a man to marry a "plain jane". Songs like, Find an Ugly Woman and Make Her Your Wife or Beauty is Only Skin Deep or Woman's Got Soul all depict a woman who may not be the "perfect 10". However, all of those songs suggest that peace and bliss will be the trade off. The "plain jane" as it relates to a woman is synonomous to the "regular joe" for a man. This type of person comes in a variety of ways and is not based solely on physical appearance. I would even argue that being a "plain jane" has just as much to do with an outlook on life or a mentality so to speak. I am referring to the woman who is happy and content with the simple pleasures of life. The woman who does not require many of life's superficial treasures and accesories to make them happy. As a R.E.A.L. man, I am often quite amazed at the amount of so called "sophisticated modern women" who suggest that those so called "plain janes" have low self esteem and do not understand what having the finer things in life are all about. I, along with many other R.E.A.L. men I know beg to differ. To us, it seems as if those plain janes have a better understanding of what makes them happy along with what will keep a man satisfied for the long term. If this is not the case then why are so many of the most gorgeous and highly educated women in the world single? (and not by choice either) Why are so many of these women in and out of relationships in less than a year? The funny thing about this is everything that you have read in this book thus far is all connected to having or not having the qualities necessary to attract a R.E.A.L. man. I break it all down in my philosophy about the guppy and the barracuda and the alpha male and alpha female. The "plain jane" seems to be winning the race and securing her future. Along the way, you should politely walk up to some woman you know or consider to fit the description of a "plain jane" and kindly ask her to tell you her secrets to being happy and content in her marriage or committed relationship with her "fine ass man"! You might just learn something useful!

Commentary 7

Money or Love

Here is the million dollar question you must ask yourself ladies. When you enter into a relationship, are you in it more for the money or for the love? If you are the type of woman who is primarily focused on the money aspect of a relationship and are caught up into having all the trappings of wealth, good luck finding a R.E.A.L. man. However, if you are interested in real love from a R.E.A.L. man and can give quality love in return, you increase your chances for a long term, committed relationship. No one is suggesting that having money is not important. I'm suggesting that it should not be the first and main criteria that is used when deciding to be in a serious relationship. A man should definitely have the means to earn a quality living and since we are talking about responsible, educated, ambitious, and loving men, making good money and having stability will more than likely come with the territory. You've all heard the saying "money can't buy love". From the Beatles to Ralph Tresvant those words have been sung from mountain high to valley low but many women just don't seem to comprehend the truth in this simple fact. I've known women more concerned with their man's occupation than how they may be treated. Many highly educated women prefer dating the corporate executive, athlete, or musician who is emotionally and physically abusive because of what he represents. Many of these women seemingly have no interest in dating a bus driver or sanitation worker because it is not a "sexy" occupation. They are too caught up with the status of things or the lack thereof. At the end of the day, when it's just you and your man, you need to decide if you love the man more than his wallet or if you love the wallet more than the man. It's all about being honest with yourself. At the end of the day, we are talking about your happiness and well being.

Commentary 8

Make A House A Home

I hate to say it ladies, but too many of you do not know how to keep house. In other words, make a house a home. There is an expression that cleanliness is next to godliness. Truer words have never been spoken or written! A R.E.A.L. man is completely turned off by a woman whose house looks like a pig sty. I've known women whose apartments looked liked a bomb hit it! The dishes were piled high up to the ceiling, garbage overflowing in the kitchen, clothes thrown all over the house and even more disgusting, roaches were jumping off the walls, out the sink, everywhere! The funny thing is that these women were all college educated, had great careers, had children, dressed impeccably and were old enough to know better. Go figure! They just lacked that knack of knowing how to keep a neat and clean house. It could have been quite possible that they just did not care enough about the overall appearance of their dwelling. BIG MISTAKE! Plain and simple ladies, men judge women very harshly and are extremely critical when it comes to this area. Honestly speaking, we see it as you having serious character flaws and will more than likely relegate you to just a "booty call" and nothing more than that. It's that severe ladies! When a R.E.A.L. man is looking to commit to a woman, he will be looking at how comfortable she makes him feel across the board. After a hard day's work and dealing with the rigors and stresses of life, the R.E.A.L.man wants to come home to a peaceful and relaxing environment. He expects and will demand that it be the place where he lays his head down and goes to sleep at night. For those of you who are somewhat challenged in this area, may I suggest you buy yourselves a few magazines to gain some insight and perspective on the subject. I would suggest O magazine, Martha Stewart Living, or any other decorative and woman based magazines from which you can draw inspiration and information from. It's never too late to embrace change. If you truly desire a R.E.A.L. man, it is imperative that you know how to keep house and make a house a home!

Commentary 9

Identifying a R.E.A.L. Man

As we come to our final commentary, I believe it is important that the woman reading this book take away the most important fact. That is, how to identify a R.E.A.L. man in the first place so you may have a quality and fulfilling relationship. Let's look at the "R" factor which stands for responsible. Before becoming deeply involved with a man, you must look to see how he is handling his current responsibilites and what his habits and tendencies are. For example, does he have multiple children with multiple women? Is he taking care of his children financially, emotionally and physcially? Does he have employment? If not, is he steadliy seeking employment? Is he paying his bills on time? Is he as I like to say "handling his business"? If the answer to all of these questions are no, then you most definitely do not want to get involved in any serious relationship with this kind of man. Now let us focus our attention on the "E" factor which stands for educated. You should find out the level and degree of education a man has before you become committed to him. Has he graduated from high school? Does he have a college degree or maybe at least some college experience? What about life experience which is also important? Has he traveled outside of his city, state or neighborhood? Does he have a certified skill or trade or a working knowledge of his craft that will allow him to earn a viable income? Is he an avid reader or a man who likes to aquire knowledge? If the answer to any of these questions are no, then it would behoove you to keep it moving. Let us now consider the "A" factor which stands for ambitious. You need to find out what motivates the man of your interest. Is he self motivated? Is he a doer or just a talker? Does he have dreams, goals and ideas? Does he have any impressive accomplishments to speak of? Does he have a plan on where he sees himself in five to ten years? Is he a leader or a follower? If a guy is a slacker, does not have a plan or a dream and lacks a sense of urgency for time and getting goals accomplished then he is the type of man you should not invest in. Lastly, let us examine the "L" factor which stands for loving. You should pay close attention to the way he deals with the other women in his life. Most importantly, how he treats his mother or daughter. Does he have a compassionate nature? Does he believe in simple romance like getting you flowers for your birthday? Is he affectionate? Can he communicate his feelings for you and towards you in an open and honest way? If the answers to these questions are no, then he is most likely not the one for you. In conclusion, all the scenarios mentioned will manifest themselves at different times in life due primarily to age and experience. Please remember to be realistic about when all of these qualities will come together in a man. A young woman should not expect a 19 year old man to have everything that a 35 year old man may have. You always have to consider that very important intangible we call *potential.* Give a good man the time, encouragement, love and support he needs and nine times out of ten he will become that R.E.A.L. man whom you can depend on and love for a lifetime!

About The Author

Bey Bright is a writer, musician, and entrepreneur. Born in New York City and raised in both New York and the Washington DC metro area, Bey spent most of his childhood and adolescent years playing sports, writing, listening to music, and entertaining the ladies. As a high school senior, he briefly enjoyed the role of sports editor for his high school newspaper. Academically, Mr.Bright excelled in and enjoyed English, Sociology, Psychology and Communications. Along with being a writer, he owns and operates a boutique entertainment company called Bright Vision Entertainment which specializes in an assortment of creative services. As a hip hop artist, writer and producer, Bey wrote and produced 4 albums,(3 rap and 1 neo soul) independently selling over 50,000 plus records to date. In 2008, Bey partnered with The Learning Annex and currently teaches an online course called How to Market, Sell, and Distribute Your Music Independently, geared towards helping independent artists and labels succeed in the music business. Mr. Bright attended Norfolk State University for one year before transferring to American InterContinental University where he would graduate and earn his BA in Business Administration. In 2008, Bey was accepted into the Masters Program at Marist College and is currently pursuing his MA in Communication.

Acknowledgements

I would like to thank and acknowledge the two most important women in my life, my beautiful wife Marcia Bright and my amazingly loving mother Regina Brown. Thank you both for all your love, support and encouragement throughout the years. As a wife Marcia, I have found in you my destiny soulmate, devoted partner and a loving foundation. Thank you for all of your support and sacrifice and thank you for being a fantastic mother to our son Marcus. Thank you Mom for raising me and laying the groundwork for me becoming a Responsible, Educated, Ambitious, Loving man. Thank you for all of your years of nurturing and for the many sacrifices you've made for me along the way. My success in life is truly an extention of your unconditional love, dedication and commitment to my well being. I'd also like to thank my son Marcus. You are my new found eternal inspiration. You have brought an enormous amount of joy and hope into my life son. My hope is that I will always have the love, dedication, discipline and commitment it takes to ensure that you become the R.E.A.L. man I write about in this book. I pray and affirm that all of God's universal blessings will be bestowed upon you and that you will remain forever blessed! Special thanks to my father Akbar "Jack" Bright for being a source of literary inspiration. Your poems, philosophies, music and life in general have helped to mold and shape my thoughts and gave me a guiding light towards my own path to manhood. Love, thanks, and respect to you always. Special thanks to my uncle Layding Bright for all of your literary and entrepreneurial inspirations. Thank you to my brother Rahsaan for all your love, teachings, advice, friendship, support and words of wisdom. Thanks to my best friends Tim Bridgwaters and John Bratcher for over 20 years of true, solid friendship and for all of our wild days and memories of chasing girls, living wild and having fun! Thanks to you both for always having my back! Much love to you both. Last but not least, I'd like to thank all of the women that passed through my life who in some form or fashion gave me the insight and experiences that allowed me to write this book. Thank you for teaching me and helping me experience love, lust, passion, loyalty, character, trust, jealousy, pain, betrayal, deceit, sacrifice, spirituality, faith, confidence, selfishness, infidelity, communication, sharing, happiness, sadness, and laughter. In the words of the immortal Al Green, love and happiness to you all!

Recommended Resources

Here are some recommended resources that I believe will be valuable to women who are interested in having a happy, healthy relationship with a R.E.A.L. man. Much of the philosophy expressed here in these resources give in my opinion, a realistic and honest break down of the exact state of affairs between men and women from an emotional and psychological standpoint. I strongly and passionately believe that these resources can also provide a greater clarity into the minds and inner feelings of R.E.A.L. men. It is also my belief that these resources could go a long way in assisting women throughout the world claim that fruitful relationship they desire and possibly teach them things about themselves that they previously may not have been aware of. My research has lead me to draw inspiration and analysis on this particular subject from all of life's many experiences. From the pastor in the church spreading the holy gospel to the retired pimps from the street corners of the inner cities of America. From comedians to authors to musicians, we can learn a great deal about life and relationships.Many times the answers and lessons to life come to us in an unorthodox and nontraditional manner. With that being said, here are Bey Bright's recommended resources for any woman serious about attracting and having a loving relationship with a R.E.A.L. man.

1. The Bible/Book of Proverbs:Author-God

I recommend reading the bible because in my opinion, the scriptures are based on the everyday foundation of life. While writing and researching for this book, I found that within the book of proverbs there are many great references and scriptures based upon good women and bad women in relation to dealing with men and the family structure. It shed light on what the character of a woman should and should not be like and can most definitely be used as a blueprint on how to not only attract a R.E.A.L. man, but how to become a better woman in general from a spritual and emotional perspective. Frankly speaking, I was quite amazed at how relevant the book of proverbs still is in today's world and how it can still be used to bring spiritual balance and a deeper committment to the family structure.

2. Save The Males: Why Men Matter Why Women Should Care: Author-Kathleen Parker

Finally! There is a woman who is brave enough to go against the grain and tell today's so called independent woman what she really needs to hear. If I had a dollar for everytime I was called a male chauvanist (sometimes, even by my own mother) for saying some of the exact same things Kathleen Parker says in her book about why men are important in a woman's life, I'd be a billionaire! I highly recommend this book simply because if gives great insight and clarity to women from another woman's perspective. I figure sometimes people need to hear the same message coming from a different messenger for a message to really sink in. Besides, the title alone was a good enough reason for me to recommend it to all of you!

3. Don'ts For Wives: Author-Blanche Ebbutt

You may find this hard to believe but, this book "Don'ts for Wives" was written in the early 1900's and the information provided is still unbelievably relevant today. Published in the United Kingdom, it is a small little pocket size book I happened to stumble across in a bookstore in Florida. This book is probably hard to find so you may want to search the internet for this one! Again, it was written by a woman who even way back then understood the real nature and psychological makeup of a R.E.A.L. man. It is literally a step by step, don't do this, don't do that kind of book for wives. As a man, I was again pleasantly surprised by the keen awareness and candor of Ms.Ebbutt and found it to be a good little resource for wives, girlfriends, etc. It is really amazing that over a century later, the nature of men and women has never changed and probably never will. So for all of my female readers squawking about the fact this recommended book is a century old and thinks it is an obsolete read for today's modern woman, just remember, men are still the same and will never change!

4. Kill The Messenger, Bring The Pain, I Think I Love My Wife:Comedian-Chris Rock

Sometimes the real heart to heart messages in life can be expressed best through humor. My main man Chris Rock needs no introduction to most of the world but for those of you who might not be familiar with him or his work, I suggest you start with watching his Bring The Pain, Kill The Messenger and I Think I Love My Wife dvds. Those two stand up performances along with the feature film delve into the deepest crevices of the male psyche. These performances by Chris Rock elaborate in great length and detail about how every man really thinks, feels and responds to a woman on every and any level. It is a no holds bard, straight no chaser kind of comedy and humor, brilliantly executed and woven into intelligent and emotionally charged comedy. They say there is always a little bit of truth in every joke. Such is the case here with the aforementioned masterpieces from Mr. Chris Rock. Don't forget to save your man the last piece of the "big chicken"!

5. Think and Grow Rich: Author-Napoleon Hill

This book is guaranteed to change your life on so many levels. I strongly recommend reading this because it goes into detail about the power and dynamics of the "Master Mind". It tells how the cooperative and sexual energies between a man and woman create a force and a bond like no other. The book also explains how the two minds more readily blend in a harmonious manner as opposed to blending minds of the same gender. Mr. Hill also suggests that the mental stimulus of a potential sexual relationship helps to create the "master mind" mentality. I believe many of you would find particularly appealing the chapters that discuss and focus on topics such as having a pleasing personality, cooperation, tolerance, concentration and self control. The benefits found in this jewel of a book will certainly aid in strenghtening a woman and her commitment not only to herself, but to her family.

6. Baisden After Dark, Love Lust & Lies Radio, Men Cry In The Dark: Author and Radio/TV Personality-Michael Baisden

What more can I say about my main man Michael Baisden? This recommended resource was a no brainer for me because I personally feel he truly understands the pulse of the people and has a daily message that women in particular can benefit from. Beyond being a true inspiration to me personally, I believe that all of Michael's platforms, his nationally syndicated radio program Love Lust & Lies, his television program Baisden After Dark or any of his books adroitly addresses the topics and concerns that all women care about from an emotional, mental and physical standpoint. What I also believe is that most women can truly benefit from Michael's philosophy and messages. Why? It is because he was a regular brother from around the way from the streets of Chicago who "came up". He still has an acute understanding and unique perspective of how the game is played and seen from the man's point of view whether that man is rich or poor, blue collar or white coller, business man or bus driver. He is a gentleman who can communicate the message of learning how to successfully deal in relationships straight to the female persuasion on every level with substance, style and sofistication.

7. Men are from Mars Women Are From Venus: Author- John Gray

Have truer words ever been spoken about men and women? Men are from Mars and women are from Venus so it seems. We all exist on planet Earth but somehow we seem to speak different languages. At least most of the time. This book is an oldie but goodie classic that should be in every woman's book collection. This is really one of the best all purpose, practical guides for improving the communication in your relationship. It emphasizes getting out of relationships what you desire to have on a consistent, long term basis. Every chapter is strongly suggested because each chapter focuses on so many important aspects of a relationship be it long term or short term. How to motivate the opposite sex, how to communicate difficult feelings, and how to ask for support and get it are the chapters in particular that give great insight and perspective. In this crazy world filled with the emotional struggles and desires for power, status, money, respect and love, this book can surely be a guiding light and sound resource to help your relationships grow and maintain a healthy balance.

8. Sex and The City Series and the Movie:Creator-Darren Star

Carrie, Miranda, Charlotte, and Samantha. I think you are all very familiar with the names. I know some of you women reading this book may be shocked that I have mentioned Sex and The City as a helpful resource. Well, Get Over It Ladies! It just so happens that I loved Sex and The City and here's why. Watching the series and movie from a male perspective gave me an opportunity to really study the psychological make up of women. What made it so great was the fact I had four totally different types of women I could really analyze and see how women make their decisions and the criteria in which those decisions are based upon. I must admit as a man, I was many times shocked and appalled, confused and apathetic to the whole damn thing. However, in the the midst of all those feelings and emotions I saw it as a guide for every woman to be able to choose what kind of man works best for them. If you think back ladies to every relationship you've ever had, many of you have been involved with at one time or another someone who shared the characteristics of the male characters from the series. You've either had a Big, an Aidan, a Steve, a Trey or a Smith Jerrod. The key here is finding which type of man works best for you and understanding what's meant for playing and what's meant for staying. Some of this I already touched on earlier in the book with my philosophy about the barracuda and the guppy. Of course however, the choice is ultimately always yours!

9. Astrological Revelations About You:
Author-Sydney Omarr

I am a firm believer that the more information you have about anything or anyone, the more successful you will be in your encounters or endeavors with that person or thing. Astrology is a science that helps people identify characteristics and personality traits of an individual. Understanding the astrological makeup of a person is crucial in determining whether or not you are truly compatible with another person and most significantly, your life partner. Many people think that astrology is a bunch of mumbo jumbo and that it has no real importance or relevance to how people get along on a long term basis. I challenge you the reader first to read the book Astrological Revelations About You. Then, I want you to begin with looking at yourself and the characteristics the book says is natural to who you are as a person based upon the date and time you were born. In an honest evaluation, judge for yourself how accurate the science of astrology is to who you are as a person now and as a child, then find out what zodiac sign your man is and see if you are compatible. I believe you will find the revelations amazing and the information and new found knowledge very useful to your relationship indeed.

10. Creative Visualization: Author-Shakti Gawain

I am a believer that to be successful in anything you have to first be able to visualize that success. Creative visualization is a process that many people have taken to over the last 20 years or so. With so many negative forces and energies that surround us in our everyday life, it is easy to become disillusioned and lose sight of our goals. Along with a strong spiritual foundation and practicing faith I have found that the act of creative visualization is a key component in the lives of successful people all over the world. Just ask Oprah Winfrey about the power and positive effects of creative visualization. In this book, Ms.Gawain teaches about the process of affirmations, healing, prosperity and a host of other positive strategies to help bring strength and balance to you and your relationships.

11. Why Did I Get Married DVD: Creator- Tyler Perry

In my opinion, this is Tyler Perry's cinematic masterpiece to date. This film depicts some of the realest and deepest messages about marriage and relationships. The film totally captures the struggles of maintaining healthy and happy relationships in the 21st century between men and women and serves as a blueprint from which we all can learn. The multiple dynamics that exist between each couple and the communication or lack thereof between those couples identify a frightening, ongoing epedemic between men and women that must be rectified before the family nucleus is further decimated by selfishness, lack of compassion, intolerance and the inability to compromise. Those of us familiar with Mr.Perry's works know he likes to tell a story that is packed with a powerful, in your face message. His film Why Did I Get Married is in my opinion, his strongest and most relevant message to date with regards to relationships between men and women. Another must have resource for your collection!

12. Act Like A Lady, Think Like A Man- Steve Harvey

Once again, we have another great comedian in Steve Harvey who was able to communicate hard, tangible information to women with a comedic flair and sofistication. This book has opened the door and set the stage for books like mine to follow and give a different spin and perspective. This book is great because it instructs women on how to think and process information like us men. It is giving you ladies a clearer understanding of why we men think like we think and react and respond to certain situations in relationships the way we do. But the most important thing to remember ladies is that we still need and want you to act like a lady at the end of the day!

13. The Godfather Part 1 & 2

This is arguably the greatest movie ever produced in the history of hollywood. If you want to see how to build and destroy a family from every perspective, you must see the Godfather, part one and part two if you have not seen it yet. The storyline is spectacular, not to mention the now legendary actors who star in this classic opus. Legendary stars Marlon Brando, Robert Deniro, Al Pacino, Robert Duvall and Diane Keaton all give heavyweight performances. Those performances go a long way in laying the work and foundation of showing how family power, unity and love is built and destroyed along the course of life. So much can be learned from this movie and it comes highly recommended!

Message in The Music

These musical gems are must hear songs that create a musical blueprint on how R.E.A.L. men think, feel and liked to be treated. The selections are diverse and worth having in your collection to better appreciate the R.E.A.L man.

1. Destiny Fulfilled-Destiny's Child (Cater To You, T-Shirt, Soldier)
2. Ryde or Die Chick- The Lox
3. If I Was Your Girlfriend- Prince
4. I Want to Pay You Back- The Chi-Lites
5. A Man's Man's Man's World- James Brown
6. Share Your World With Me- Aretha Franklin
7. Make Yours a Happy Home- Gladys Knight & The Pips
8. Giving Him Something He Can Feel- En Vogue/Aretha Franklin
9. I've Got So Much Love To Give- Barry White
10. Around The Way Girl- LL Cool J
11. You're All I Need- Marvin Gaye &TammiTerrell/ Method Man & Mary J Blige
12. Love, Need & Want You- Patti LaBelle
13. If You Don't Know Me By Now- Harold Melvin & The Blue Notes/Simply Red
14. Ordinary People- John Legend
15. Heart of A Woman- R Kelly
16. I Will Always Love You- Whitney Houston
17. 21 Questions- 50 Cent
18. If You Think You're Lonely Now- Bobby Womack
19. Think It Over- The Delfonics
20. Be Without You- Mary J. Blige

Examples of R.E.A.L. Men in Mainstream Society

1. Barack Obama
2. Denzel Washington
3. Will Smith
4. Malcolm X
5. Percy Miller (Master P)
6. Bill Gates
7. Bill Cosby
8. Colin Powell
9. Tim Russert
10. Cal Ripken Jr.
11. Hank Aaron
12. Jackie Robinson

Examples of R.E.A.L. Women in Mainstream Society

1. Jackie Kennedy
2. Coretta Scott King
3. Rachel Robinson
4. Hillary Clinton
5. Melinda Gates
6. Maria Shriver
7. Jada Pinkett Smith
8. Beyonce Knowles
9. Oprah Winfrey
10. Nicole Kidman

Questionnaire #1

Are you worthy of a R.E.A.L. man?

Many women think that they are deserving of a good man. A prince charming. As a barometer of where you are as a "good woman", answer these questions honestly to see if you have what it takes to attract a R.E.A.L. man. If you do not possess at least 90 percent of these qualities, chances are you have some major work to do on yourself before that R.E.A.L. man comes knocking at your door.

1. Are you a nurturer?
2. Are you naturally self sacrificing?
3. Are you loyal?
4. Are you supportive?
5. Do you have a sense of humor?
6. Do you have common sense?
7. Are you sexually adventurous?
8. Are you a positive person?
9. Do you maintain your physical apperance?
10. Are you a compassionate person?
11. Are you a good cook?
12. Can you make a house a home?
13. Are you educated?
14. Are you an honest person?
15. Are you a great listener?

Questionnaire #2
How Important Is Sex To You

Most R.E.A.L. men require a healthy and active sex life. They need the sex to be on point and for the woman to be open to unconventional ways of love making. To see if you are sexually compatible with a R.E.A.L. man, answer the following questions as honestly as possible.

1. How much do you love sex?
2. Are you sexually experienced?
3. Are you sexually creative?
4. Do you have any sexual hang ups?
5. Are you sexually inhibited?
6. How much do you enjoy oral sex? (giving and receiving)
7. Do you enjoy anal sex?
8. Do you enjoy role playing?
9. Are you into sexy lingerie?
10. Are you into adult entertainment?

Love Vocabulary Words

Here are some words I feel are essential to know the true meaning of. I would ask all of my readers to look up each word listed in the dictionary and truly grasp the meanings so that it may be a a resourceful reminder of how to keep your relationships strong and viable.

1. Love
2. Committment
3. Respect
4. Patience
5. Loyalty
6. Benevolance
7. Sacrifice
8. Humor
9. Nurture
10. Lady
11. Woman
12. Mother
13. Wife
14. Communication
15. Tolerance
16. Giving
17. Spirituality
18. Sharing
19. Romance
20. Chivalry

Additional Products From Bey Bright and
Bright Vision Entertainment

1. Tia Dae- "It's A Nu Dae" (neo soul/jazz music) available on iTunes, CDBaby.com & Amazon.com

If you enjoy neo soul, smooth jazz, and rhythm & blues, then this cd is a must have and will serve as a nice addition to your music collection! Think Erykah Badu meets Mary J. Blige and Anita Baker!

2. FlamBey- "Destiny & The Flamerous Life" (hip hop music) available on iTunes, CDBaby.com, Rhapsody and Amazon.com

Hip Hop music with a classic new school/old school flavor. FlamBey's style has been coined "Gangsta Sexy" and the subject matter is most definately smooth for the ladies and hard enough for the fellas. Standout songs include Hot Girl, That's What She's Lookin For, On & Poppin and Gangsta Luv and Destiny (remix).

Please visit our website at www.BrightVisionEnt.com and connect with Bey Bright on FaceBook and LinkedIn.

For bookings and interviews with Bey Bright please call 917 991-1906 or email us at BeyBright@gmail.com and feedback@ brightvisionent.com.